The Simple Side Of

Human Resource Management

Managing people should not be difficult, boring or scary

Jan H Pieterse

For more information, material and advice on many of the topics surrounding management functions go to:

www.NextCEO.co.za

Copyright © 2016 by Jest My Publishing.

All Rights Reserved. No part of this publication may be reproduced in any form or by any means, including scanning, photocopying, or otherwise without prior written permission of the copyright holder.

Additional Action

Go join our Facebook group for exclusive offers, group collaboration, coaching and other great benefits at NextCEOGroupCaching or follow our Facebook page for general information and motivation NextCEO.co.za

Why I Wrote This Book

I wrote this book because, I felt that in so many cases where people do research studies and/or research papers in general, either for self-enrichment or as part of a study purpose towards a certified outcome, these research papers seem to get lost in the cracks. During my studies I came across a philosophy that stated that; A scholar during their undergraduate degree, merely summarizes and compares the knowledge from the greater pool of knowledge, whereas a scholar studying towards a master degree, searches and tests these collections of knowledge and verifies the information in the greater pool of knowledge, whereas, the Ph.D. scholar is the one that contributes and grows the pool of knowledge.

For many years I believed this philosophy, however, as time passed I realized that even the least expectant individual can significantly contribute to the knowledge pool and feed the inquisitiveness of the information hungry souls. Thus I have decided it a fitting choice to publish the research that I had done for the various business projects during my studies. I can only hope that you would not only find this information useful but that you find the book enjoyable.

Why You Should Read This Book

If you are interested in understanding human resource management in greater detail, but you are just not in the mood for those stale academic written, hard to understand, boring textbooks, then this book is just for you.

If you are simply looking for additional information and wish to supplement your existing knowledge on human resource management, well then this book is for you.

For the sake of covering both angles, this book includes the academic writing, as well as simpler written interpretations of the same information. The non-academic people amongst us, or simply those who will benefit from a simpler side of things can benefit none the less.

With a pinch of salt, a dash of garnish, this book will help you understand some of the in-depth parts of the human resource management paradigm.

You may at some parts feel that you have completely lost your way, but fear not. As I have, and many before us, you will survive the journeys into the paradigms of the business management empire.

TABLE OF CONTENTS

Additional Action 2
Why I Wrote This Book 2
Why You Should Read This Book 3
Table of Contents 4
Understanding the Book 6
Human Resource Management Functions 6
Roles and Responsibilities of a human resource manager 7
The purpose of developing a human resource plan 10
Recruitment techniques during recruitment and selection .. 12
Stages of team development 15
Effective communication in leadership and management 17
Developing and implementing a training plan 18
Performance appraisal feedback methods 21
Human Resource Management in perspective 23
Human Resource Lifecycle 23
Human Capital Management 26
Differentiate Workforce Planning vs. Human Resource Planning 27
Importance of Workforce Gap Analysis 29
Succession Planning 31
Link between Strategic Plans and Job Description 34
Difference between Remuneration and Reward 36
Appropriateness of reward systems for motivating employees 38

Benefits of a Well-Functioning Performance Management Process 40

Links between Performance Appraisal and Career Development..43

About The Author 45

Other Books By Jan H Pieterse 46

Understanding the Book

The standard text such as this will contain academic style writing with citations and arguments. This is where the facts are defined in great detail. If you prefer to read the fact in their original context, I have included a bibliography at the end of this book for your perusal.

The highlighted text such as this is aimed at the audience that wishes to have a simpler understanding of the topic, and in a way that can simply be retold or re-quoted easily.

Human Resource Management Functions

Human Resource Management, the golden trio. No other form of management includes such an in-depth and critical involvement with both the human element as well as the capital resource that is represented by the human skills, experience, and capability.

The term 'Human Resource Development' was introduced to the 1969 Miami Conference of the American Society of Training and Development by Leonard Nadler.[1]

ROLES AND RESPONSIBILITIES OF A HUMAN RESOURCE MANAGER

The human resource manager performs an integral part of an organization, especially related to the employees. The human resource manager has many critical roles. Some of these are compensation, hiring, performance management, organization development, safety, wellness, benefits, employee motivation, communication, administration, and training[2].

Simply:

The human resource manager does a lot of things relating to the employees in the organization. The areas that are generally covered are: Salaries, rewards, employee hiring and firing, making sure employees work hard, ensuring company becomes better, ensuring employees are safe, happy, healthy, and other benefits, ensuring employees are motivated, ensuring that employees know what is expected, lots of admin, ensuring employees become smarter.

These roles all form part of an organization's human resource plan and strategy. The following list explains some of these roles in more detail:

Compensation and benefits; Compensation refers to **all** forms of financial returns, tangible services and benefits employees receive as part of an employment relationship.[3]

Hiring (recruiting); Hiring can be defined as acquiring of sufficient numbers of applicants to apply for the various jobs in the business as and when required.[4]

Performance management; an ideal performance appraisal involves the comparison of work results with quantitative objectives.[4]

Development; has a long-term focus on preparing for future work responsibilities, while at the same time increasing the capacities of the employees to perform their current jobs.[4]

Well-being (Safety, Wellness, Motivation); Employees need to be better motivated, not only to improve organizational effectiveness but also to provide a better quality of life for all employees.[4]

Communication; can be regarded as part of the backbone of an organization, and can be integrated into many of the roles of an HR manager. Communication is vital for employees to understand what is expected in their day to day tasks. Manager's decisions are based on communication from employees.

Training; Training typically involves providing employees with the knowledge and skills needed to do a particular task or job.[4]

The roles and responsibilities of an HR manager are extensive in an organization, however; both human resource specialists and line managers are responsible for managing the people talent in organizations.[4] Therefore many of these roles can be delegated to line managers as in most cases they have a closer working relationship with the employees and their tasks.

Simply:

There as 7 (seven) core roles in human resource management, these include:

Compensation; Giving the money, leave options, medical, dental, stock options, and throw in a car.
Hiring; Reading résumés, interviewing and telling people they are hired.
Performance; performance measurement makes sure that every employee can work hard and complete their tasks.
Development; let the employees get better at what they do, and aspire to get promoted.
Well-being and Safety; Employees should be kept safe and motivated to be most effective in their jobs.
Communication; Communicating effectively with employees is one of the most important roles. Always communicate with personnel as this helps heightened morale.
Training; Training employee makes them feel valued and smarter, which generally leads to increased productivity.

The Purpose of Developing a Human Resource Plan

A critical task in the paradigm of a human resource manager is to ensure that a human resource plan is defined to reflect the human resource needs of the organization. Human resource planning is sometimes referred to as workforce planning, is the process of forecasting the organization's human resource needs. The human resource plan needs to align with the organization's goals and strategy. The topics addressed in the human resource plan needs to include, but is not limited to recruiting, hiring, training and developing a sustainable workforce.[4]

Developing a human resource plan in a systematic manner will enhance productivity, consistency and customer service and will also pave the way for optimal interaction between your staff and new technology an organization plans to adopt.[5]

The human resource plan can be divided into the following three steps[4]:

- Identifying the current jobs being done in the organization by means of job analysis and defining job descriptions.

- Identifying the type of employees required to do the work by means of a job specification.

- Identifying the future employee requirements of the organization by means of forecasting and planning.

The outcome of the human resource plan will be providing structured guidelines that will indicate how the organizations short-, medium- and long-term human resource requirements can be provided for.[4]

Simply:

One does not simply just hire and fire. It is important to have a plan, especially a plan regarding which employees you need to do the right jobs. Employee planning can be done as the organization progresses and grows.

The three basic steps to planning an organization's employee needs are:

1. Analyze what jobs need to be done. Build the job descriptions for each of them.

2. What skills are needed to do these jobs? Amend the job descriptions based on the scope of skills.

3. Will you need other employees in future? If you want to grow, you will yes. Start planning for these positions.

Recruitment techniques during recruitment and selection

The purpose of recruitment is to ensure a sufficient amount of applicants apply for an existing or planned job vacancy. Recruitment techniques available to the human resource manager are as follows:

Advertising; placing an advertisement in newspapers and magazines is regarded as the most common form of recruiting[4]. The advantage of this technique is that a full specification can be published to avoid incorrect applications.

Consultants and labor agencies; this technique is very useful for smaller organizations which don't have an HR department. This technique saves the organization valuable time as only the most correct candidates are referred by the agencies. This technique can become costly as many agencies charge recruitment fees.

Employee referrals; Requesting employees to recruit acquaintances to apply for positions can save money on other recruitment techniques, however, this technique can also result in staff conflict if one employee's acquaintance is appointed instead of another, however, recruitment costs are kept low.

Personal approach; Often referred to as head hunting, this technique is more often used when the job vacancy requires a specialized skill. In most cases, the candidate is known to management and the recruiter has a good understanding of the person's skills and abilities.

Internet; There are many sites available today to aid in recruitment, some sites general across all sectors of the market and some specific to a sector of the market[6].

Sundry strategies; Organizations often use visits to schools and universities with long-term objectives in mind[4.] This technique could include bursaries, internship program or just introduction of the organization and the opportunities it offers.

These techniques all have their advantages and disadvantages. It will, therefore, be beneficial to an organization to adopt multiples of these techniques. Other reasons for diversifying recruitment techniques is that in most cases there are only two types of people looking at job advertisements, those who are out of work, and those looking to change jobs. They roughly represent 10 – 15% of the workforce available out there[6].

Placing adverts on the internet for unskilled workers would be much less efficient than using a labor agency targeted at that sector in the market, therefore finding the best technique is highly dependent on the sector of the market that the organization is recruiting for.

Simply:

If you are looking for more employees, there are 6 key methods that you can apply.

Advertise in local media, as this has been the default and most effective way in the past, but let us be fair, this is the information age, and this is no longer the most effective way. In most cases, this is a very cheap option.

Contact employment agencies to recruit for you, as they have done most of the hard work and there is most likely an agency that specializes in the specific skills that you need. Agencies need to make money as well, and thus they charge fees. This could range between a small once off fee, up to a percentage of the new recruit's annual remuneration. In high-end markets, this can turn out to be a very large price tag.

Ask the existing employees to refer their friends who are in the same industry, this could be the cheapest option, however in many cases organizations offer placement fees if a referral was successfully employed.

You could directly headhunt employees that you have been scouting for some time, especially when you are seeking specialist skills.

The internet has turned into the most effective sourcing method, as many individuals have registered portfolios on various websites focused at recruiters, or just as a strategic personal web presence. Additionally, there are countless websites available within each market sector for advertising available positions.

Internships and scholarships are handy methods to scout and introduce young new recruits into the organization. New employees are usually much cheaper than established professionals; however, they lack the knowledge that comes with experience.

Stages of team development

Team development is one of the aspects in the development and wellbeing roles within human resource management. It is important for the human resource manager to ensure that employees function well in teams, as well functioning teams equates to positive production outcomes.

Team development can be categorized into 5 stages according to Bruce Tuckman's theory[7, 8].

Forming; this stage is where the group is formed and usually filled with confusion with regards to the goals of the team and the individual's roles within that team[7]. This is the stage where people get to know each other and goals and processes are established[8]. The roles of the leader in this stage of development will be to facilitate team-building, defining the process and needs to understand the needs of the team[7].

Storming; in this stage the team will see conflicts between members, as trust amongst members is low, and power struggles are visible. Concerns and criticism are often voiced at this stage. At this point, the team will either disband or continue. The role of the leader in this stage of development is to facilitate patience and tolerance between members and guide the team towards their common goal, roles, and processes.

Norming; at this stage the team starts to develop work habits and support structures and cohesion starts to form in the team. Trust starts forming and communication barriers start diminishing. The team starts to deliver positive results and is focused on the common goals. At this stage, the leader will encourage communication and participation of team members.

Performing; at this stage, the team has matured and shown high levels of loyalty and participation of members and group decision making as well as conflict resolution. The team reaches a point of being self-managed, as the focus of common goals drives the team. The leader in this stage facilitates an efficient communication process and supports when the team risks reverting to prior stages.

Adjourning; this is the stage where the finalizing of the team's efforts are affected and team achievements are recognized. This stage is commonly associated with levels of mourning and feelings of closure. Not all teams will reach this stage as some teams are regarded as relatively permanent. The role of leadership in this stage is to emphasize the achievement of the team and gratitude of stakeholders.

Simply:

When attempting to establish a team to execute tasks collectively, there are 5 stages that these teams progress through as part of a well-functioning team lifecycle.

Forming – The group gets together and roles and goals are not yet established.

Storming – The egos will challenge each other for authority and direction

Norming – Stability and hierarchy start to form

Performing – The team functions as a collective force and production levels are at optimal levels

Adjourning – The tasks are complete and the team disbands to possibly form other teams

EFFECTIVE COMMUNICATION IN LEADERSHIP AND MANAGEMENT

Studies of how much time managers spend on various activities show that communication occupies 70 to 90 percent of their time every day[63,10]. This in itself emphasizes the importance of effective communication in leadership and management. Leadership needs communication to effectively guide employees in their day to day tasks, to motivate staff on any levels and to inspire others in their communication skills as leaders are the influencers of an organization. Communication either has the power to strengthen or to weaken the organization's morale and purpose[9, 10].

It is important for leaders to provide direction to employees, by communicating the vision of the organization and clearly and effectively laying out the organization's guidelines and boundaries and encouraging the employees to give feedback on their thoughts, opinions, and concerns. The leader needs to enforce communication with employees by constructively replying to the feedback[9].

The individual who gets ahead in business is the person who "is able to communicate, to make sound decisions, and to get things done with and through people" – Bowman[10]

Simply:
Leadership and effective communication go hand in hand. It is critical for an organization's optimal performance that managers communicate well with the employees. Managers

should not only walk the walk, but they should talk the talk. They should lead by example.

DEVELOPING AND IMPLEMENTING A TRAINING PLAN

The basic systematic model emphasizes that training and development should be undertaken on a planned basis as a result of a logical series of steps[11]. In practice, the number and description of these steps tend to differ, some of these steps include:

Development of training plan purpose; in this step, it is important for the HR manager to determine the purpose of the plan, by identifying the training and development needs of the employees for the current and future wellbeing of the organization.

Identification of training and development needs; is in itself probably the most important step of the plan, as the accuracy of this step will result in sustainable and achievable development outcomes.

This step can be further broken into sub-steps:

- Determining the key tasks of employee groups required to perform their job functions optimally based on the job description developed for the specific position.

- Determining competencies required by the employees to perform their tasks. This step can be delegated to the line managers.

- Determining the current state of skills and competencies of the workforce. This task can be delegated down to the line manager and it is important to involve the employee to rate themselves in these skills and competencies, as the line manager is not always aware of the scope of the skills and competencies that the employees have.

- Assessing the outcomes of the reports from the line managers, in order to effectively develop the training and development plan.

Simply:

To identify the need for training, there are a couple of steps that can be followed:

Analyze the needs of the organization. Identify the tasks that need to be performed. Identify the skills required to complete these tasks. Identify these skills in the currently available pool of skills. Review the gap between the skills pool and skills requirement, and propose training.

Development of training objectives and plans; the plan is developed based on the prioritized results of the assessments of all the departments of the organization, and a training and development budget is established based on this plan.

Implementation of planned training; this step has a longer term goal than the development of the training and development plan. However, an organization's training plan needs to often be revised to establish new needs and requirements in training. The HR department needs to take steps to implement and monitor the execution and monitoring of the plan in order to establish its effectiveness.

Evaluation and review of training; the HR department needs to annually monitor and review the training and assesses whether in-house training conforms to expected national standards.

Simply:

There are 5 core steps to developing and implementing a training plan:

1. Develop the purpose of the plan
2. Identify the training need
3. Develop training objective and plans
4. Implementation of the planned training
5. Evaluate and review the training

There is a common pattern that can be found in most aspects of management, Identify need, Analyze, Identify solutions, Select the best solution, Implement, Assess impact, Repeat. It is truly as simple as that.

PERFORMANCE APPRAISAL FEEDBACK METHODS

Of the many performance appraisal methods available, they all have one main objective to collect feedback from elected human or non-human sources regarding the performance of a specific employee. Examples of feedback methods are:

360-degree feedback; provides the employee the opportunity to receive feedback from a selection of his or her co-workers, supervisor, customers, suppliers and themselves. This method enables the employee to understand how his or her effectiveness as an employee is viewed by others. People, who are selected as raters, should be choices shared by both the employee and the organization and generally interact directly with the employee. Some debates that arise from this method are whether the feedback should be anonymous, face-to-face or independently submitted. One must also take into consideration that human perception in not an exact science, especially as a result of the halo effect, where the judgment of somebody can be affected by each person's own overall impression of the individual[12, 13, 14].

Weighted checklists; (rating scale) provides a way for an employee to be graded on a number of statements based on his or her job description and specification. These statements are grouped and weighted respective to the group and each group, in turn, is weighted towards the final result[15]. This method consists of direct, but limited, measures such as sales figures, production numbers, the electronic performance monitoring of data entry workers, etc[16]. This method deals with a wide scope of criteria, however, it can be inaccurate as the variability in an employee's performance could relate to factors beyond his or her control[16]. A further downfall of this method is that it is very extensive and time-consuming.

The two listed methods above explain the diversity available for organizations to use in performance appraisals, however, each option has its downfalls, and it would be beneficial to an organization to introduce an appraisal feedback method that amalgamates these two methods for an even more accurate reflection of the performance of an individual employee.

Simply:

The focus is mainly biased towards the two most common review methods in the industry at the moment.

360-degree feedback – employees are rated by their colleagues, as well as managers, this projects a holistic picture of the employee's performance.

Weighted checklist – Employees are scored against various predefined deliverables based on the employee's respective job description

Human Resource Management in Perspective

Human Resource Management can be perceived from many angles, and no matter which perspective you approach it from, at some point, you will enter into the same lifecycle. Human resource lifecycle affords managers a holistic view of the processes involved in human resource management.

Human Resource Lifecycle

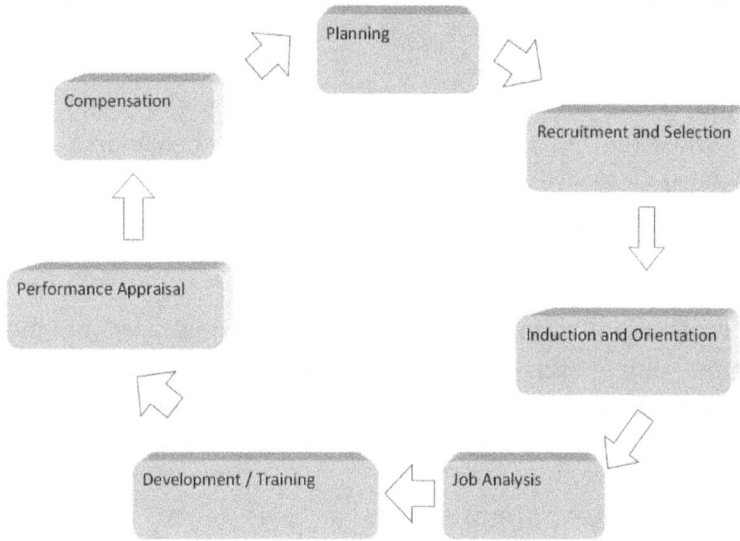

Human Resource Planning (HRP); refers to the on-going systematic planning of human resources to ensure the most optimal match between job and employee while balancing the current supply vs. the demand as well as the projected supply and demand[17]. Planning is a continuous task catering for the short and long term. HRP aims to link human resource management directly to the strategic plan of the organization[18].

Recruitment; includes planning for the position through passive or active sourcing of candidates. Posting job vacancy ads in newspapers or online. Screening interested candidates to ensure they fit the requirement. Interviews with candidates for shortlisting to determine fit for the position. Hiring successful candidates based on the outcomes of interviews and salary negotiations[19].

Induction; is the process of combining people, processes, and technology needed to optimize the effect that a new employee has on business outcomes[20]. Induction helps employees to familiarize themselves with the job and the organization[20, 21].

Job Analysis; refers to the procedure of collecting information, describing verifiable job behaviors and activities. The procedure to determine the duties and skills required as well as the kind of person required for a specific job[21, 22].

Training; Training and development for part of the foundation of each employees path with the organization and ensures that the workforce fulfills the needs of the organization[23].

Performance Appraisal; is a review and discussion process of an employee's performance based on a set of duties and responsibilities. The appraisal measures skills and accomplishments and helps to identify areas for enhancement and promotion of personal growth[24]. Performance appraisal has many benefits to the organization, management, and the employees. These benefits include promotion, compensation, development, validation, communication, and motivation[23].

Compensation; reward usually in the form of money that an organization pays to an employee for work done over a given period[25].

Simply:

The human resource life cycle follows the following steps:

Human Resource Plan – This is the ongoing plan to assess the employee requirements of the organization.

Recruitment – The process of looking for and employing staff for the available positions in the organization

Induction – This is the process of introducing employees to the organization and its strategy, and processes.

Job analysis – identify what needs to be done on the job, these include the duties and skills required

Training – ensure that employee's skills and knowledge are kept up to date and relevant with industry expectation.

Performance appraisal - review employee's performance either via 360 or via scorecard, as employees anticipating review generally are more productive

Compensation- money or rewards for work done.

HUMAN CAPITAL MANAGEMENT

Human capital management focuses more on the value that each employee contributes to the organization and can be perceived as assets[26]. The current value of a human asset can be calculated and enhanced through investment, and should have clearly defined performance expectations[27] and is a strategic approach to people management that focuses on issues critical to the organization's success. The most useful contribution of human capital to date is in defining the link between human resources and business strategy. The idea of human capital management as follows: 'A human capital approach implies that a realistic business strategy must be informed by human capital data. In other words, how can a business pursue a strategy that doesn't take account of the capacity of all the resources available, including the human ones?'[28] The term 'human capital' is defined as 'the contribution of people [their skills and knowledge] in the production of goods and services[29].

Simply:
Human capital defines the capital value that the collective skills and knowledge of the employees offer to the organization. The value that the skills of the people and the output of these skills offer the organization is often ignored or just not valued enough by managers. If it was not for the expert skills and experience of these employees, the organization would not be able to perform as optimal as it should.

DIFFERENTIATE WORKFORCE PLANNING VS. HUMAN RESOURCE PLANNING

There are different terms used to refer to the process by which organizations plan to ensure that their human resources are applied in a way that best serves that organization. This process is most often referred to as human resource planning[23], however also referred to as workforce planning defined as "a systematic, yet dynamic process of estimating the future demand for and supply of employees to execute the organization's work in ways that will best support its strategic direction, and deciding how to align and match them[30]." Thus human resource planning aims to link human resource management directly to the strategic plan of the organization. Including dealing with structure, competencies, accountability, organization, and leadership required to make the strategy work[31].

Workforce planning is about the right talent with the right skills, at the right time and at the right cost, to deliver on short and long term organizational objectives and to support the organizational strategy, which pertains to the strategic response to the changing in the workforce demographics, business models and economics[32, 33]. The on-going systematic planning of human resources can ensure the most optimal match between job and employee and includes the process of balancing the current supply versus the demand as well as the projected supply and demand and is a continuous task catering for the short and long term[17].

Simply:

Workforce planning is about the right talent with the right skills, at the right time and at the right cost, to deliver on short and long term organizational objectives

Human Resource Planning aims to ensure that an organization has the right people at the right place at the right time, all the time.

IMPORTANCE OF WORKFORCE GAP ANALYSIS

The importance of a workforce gap analysis is regarded as a critical step in the scope of workforce analysis. This is evident in the highlighting of the actual purpose of gap analysis.

The process of conducting a gap analysis for human resources gives the leaders of the organization a reading on future employment needs by identifying required competencies for their and the organization's vision and budget and comparing those projected human resources requirements to the current workforce[34]. Additionally, this process helps provide clarity to the key focus areas of Human Resource Management, which are critical to support the goals and achievements of the organization[35]. The workforce gap analysis process can be defined as the difference between what needs to be done, versus what is currently being done, and further illustrates the formula[36]:

f(gap) = (as is) − (to be)

Consequently, conducting a gap analysis can reveal information or solutions that could save an organization thousands in unwanted fines, fees, claims and indirect costs[37].

The additional benefits of a workforce gap analysis to be as follows[38]:

- Ability to identify needs for further education of employees.
- Ability to identify a better match between skill sets and available job positions.
- Ability to promote career growth opportunities earlier to employees.
- Identify opportunities to promote internships for students.
- Ability to establish additionally promotable skills.
- Develop a job migration strategy.

By understanding the workforce, it enables proper human resource planning and management in relation to business goals and planning[39].

The importance of conducting the workforce gap analysis show strong evidence in favor of the benefits of the process and conclusively highlights the importance of conducting a workforce gap analysis.

Simply:

A gap is determined by comparing the future planned state against the current state.

Thus, GAP = CURRENT - FUTURE

This allows managers to know if employees need to be trained, whether employees can be cross utilized in available positions, whether employees can be promoted, develop opportunities for job migration.

> If a manager knows what he has in employees and skills, then he is much more likely to understand the potential of the team.

SUCCESSION PLANNING

The implementation and execution of a succession plan can minimize the challenges caused by skills departure from an organization. The benefits of succession planning can be defined as:

Succession planning has been described as: "a process whereby an organization ensures that employees are recruited and developed to fill each key role within the company. Through your succession planning process, you recruit superior employees, develop their knowledge, skills, and abilities, and prepare them for advancement or promotion into ever more challenging roles."[39] Succession planning is a way to retain high-performing employees. To effectively implement succession planning, the organization's long-term goals need to be identified[23]. The importance of succession planning is highlighted in the following reasons[40]:

- Organizations can plan better for disaster
- Used to build stronger employee and department relationships
- Gives the succeeding employee a voice
- Ability for the organization to plan for the bigger picture
- Generally, can improve the morale of employees based on career development options

Key focus areas as in succession planning should include the following[41]:

- Address employee needs for when senior management retire or leave

- Preparation for unexpected or undesirable events

- Ensure that the organization has the right people in place now and in the future

- Enabling the organization to support the current culture going forward

- Helps define the sustainability of the business strategy and organization goals

However, there are common mistakes that are made by organization when conducting succession planning[42]:

1. Assuming that success at one level will guarantee success at a higher level

2. Assuming that managers are the best judges of who is promotable

3. Assuming that promotions are rewards

4. Trying to do too much too fast

5. Giving no thought to naming the process

6. Assuming that Everyone wants a promotion

The key purpose of Succession Planning is to ensure the stability of tenure in personnel. Henri Fayol argued that it is the responsibility of management to "ensure the stability of tenure of personnel", and that if that need is ignored, that key positions will end up being filled with "ill-prepared" people.

Simply:

Succession Planning is the sustained systematic efforts to ensure that the right people will be in the right places and at the right times to do the right things so as to achieve the right results[43].

This is especially critical for key employees such as executive staff, strategic staff and key individuals with a specialized skill. This could include individuals specialized knowledge individuals such as equipment specialist with contained knowledge, Sales staff with in-depth knowledge of client details, and skills.

LINK BETWEEN STRATEGIC PLANS AND JOB DESCRIPTION

In order to establish the link between strategic plans and a job description, the link between job analysis and strategic planning will first have to be established, and as a job description is a critical part of job analysis, the critical link will be proved.

During the process of developing an organization, the organization enters into the process of job analysis, which is the development of positions that the organization will need to fulfill its needs to complete its mission and to reach its vision. Job analysis is a critical part of the organization's strategic solution, as it defines the need for human resources which will be used throughout the organization. The process of job analysis includes collecting and assembling job-related information in order to design a corporate strategy that aids human resource managers to determine which resources to target and how to fill specific vacancies[44]. The main objective of job analysis is to understand who fits into what job, whereas strategic planning determines how to use human capital to achieve organizational goals[45].

A job description is based on the objective information that is obtained through the job analysis and is defined based on the competencies and skills needed for the task which in turn is needed for the organization to fulfill its goals[2]. The job description is further linked to the strategic objectives of an organization to ensure a position being recruited for is relevant to the needs of the organization[23].

The final step in the job analysis work-flow is developing of the job description and job specification and is the only tangible products of job analysis.

Simply:

The strategic plan for the organization defines where and how the organization is planning to achieve its goals, thus within this strategic plan, there should be a part that explains what it is that the organization is going to be doing, what services or products will be offered. These areas then lead to the job analysis which defines what work needs to be done, and which skills are required to do the work.

With the job analysis in hand, managers can easily formulate job descriptions based on the strategic grouping of the various skill sets, and identify targeted resources.

DIFFERENCE BETWEEN REMUNERATION AND REWARD

Remuneration, commonly known as "pay", often includes benefits or indirect remuneration, while rewards are more reserved to refer to incentives that are received, over and above the fixed remuneration. Remuneration is related to the job, while rewards are usually related to performance[23].

However, there are no universal applicable meaning attached to these terms. All monetary and non-monetary benefits that an employee receives in return for their services are generally referred to as compensation or reward for employment. Variable performance-based payments are sometimes referred to under names such as incentives or commission, and in many cases organizations refer to all monetary payments towards employees as pay systems. In some cases, the term "reward" is used to refer to cases of recognition of special achievement[46].

The term remuneration has a broad-based meaning that represents all the ways in which an employee is compensated for his or her role within an organization, including a salary, rewards, incentives, bonuses, stocks and any other paid for benefits. The term remuneration can be traced back hundreds of years to the year 1477 AD and the original Latin word "remuneration", literally meaning "a repaying" or reward for goods and services[47].

Simply:

The difference between remuneration and rewards in many cases is vague and not definitively defined, yet there seems to be a general association of these words in the human resources paradigm, which associates remuneration with the complete fully inclusive package and reward as a subset of remuneration pertaining to an incentive. Remuneration is the whole lot combined; the blanket statement that covers all forms of reward, pay, benefits, and the reward is part of the composition of remuneration.

Appropriateness of Reward Systems for Motivating Employees

Rewards systems have long been used as a form of motivation, the effectiveness of this practice is disputable based on certain factors and scenarios at play.

In a study, psychologists had established that rewards resulted in a reduction in performance especially when the performance involved creativity. This study found that: "the sense that something is worth doing for its own sake, typically declines when someone is rewarded for doing it". Thus, as a result, the psychologist feared that organizations might be diminishing interest and discouraging innovation amongst employees by administering intrinsic motivation[48]. Similar studies have found that young children who are rewarded for drawing, are less likely to draw on their own than children who draw just for the fun.

However, in a more recent neurophysiology study[49], it was revealed that neurons in certain parts of the brain carry specific signals about the past and future rewards and that these dopamine neurons display a near immediate reward signal indicating the difference between actual and predicted rewards. The study also found that these neurons are important for developing behavioral patterns. Additional to the dopamine neurons, other neurons are formed in respective locations across the brain which identify and anticipate rewards, resulting in organizing "goal-directed" behavior. These different neuron signals complement each other. This study goes so far as to compare reward systems to the use of certain forms of narcotics.

For companies to neglect employee benefits and rewards might reflect well on the company's balance sheets, however, it could have disastrous results on the hiring, retention, and long-term employee success. Rewards and recognition convey ideas of distinguishing and motivation to employees, and when these reward systems are applied correctly, they can aid the organization in achieving its mission and goals[50].

Maslow's hierarchy of needs can be taken into consideration in support of reward system as a form of motivation[51]. In Maslow's hierarchy of needs, level 4 addresses the need for "Esteem", the need for them to feel good about themselves. The most important tool in this area is the "judicious use of praise". "feelings of being recognized". When certain specifiable conditions exist, reward systems have proven to motivate performance[52]. These conditions can be; the importance that "rewards must be perceived to be tied in a timely fashion to effective performance"

Simply:

A reward can be an effective form of motivation, as long as the correct conditions exist, namely: correct timing and targeted at performance and not mere participation.

Studies have found that some effective reward systems can be compared to the use of certain narcotics, in the neurological effects that it has on people.

Benefits of a Well-Functioning Performance Management Process

The benefits of a well-functioning performance managing system (PMS) are indicated in many articles and proven in many survey studies across the globe[53].

These studies have shown that a PMS can improve an organization's sales and profit, and reduce overheads by as much as 25%. PMS can be linked to improvements in return on assets, and even linked to customer and employee satisfaction. Well-functioning performance management system plays a crucial role in improving the overall organizational performance through the management of a team and individual performance targeted at achieving organizational goals[54].

Organizational benefits of a PMS include[53]:

- Employees focused on organizational goals
- Employee retention
- Improved productivity
- Performance aligned with strategy
- Customer satisfaction
- Operational goals align with strategic objectives

Not only is the organization a benefactor from PMS, but there specific employee benefits to a well-functioning PMS, some of which include[55]:

- Security in job expectancy
- Anticipated rewards
- Visual on own performance
- Awareness of the ability to self-improve
- Improved morale

There are additional positive influences on the job satisfaction and employee loyalty, these influences include transparency, a link between performance and reward, clear established objectives and opportunities for career growth[54].

However, in order to ensure a successful PMS implementation, it not only takes hard work, rigor, and discipline[56]. There are a couple of demerits to PMS, namely that it is time-consuming, costly, complex, potentially misleading, and discouraging to intuition and monotonous[53]. PMS is known as the "Achilles' heel" of human capital management, and it is regarded as the most difficult human resource system to implement in an organization[57]. Employee management is often ranked as the lowest rated area in employee satisfaction surveys; however performance management systems are the primary driver for production performance[57].

Simply:

The benefits of a well-functioning performance management system notably outweigh the disadvantages of such a system.

The organization benefits include, employees focused on organizational goals, employee retention, improved productivity, performance aligned with strategy, customer satisfaction, and operational goals align with strategic objectives

The employee's benefits include security in job expectancy, anticipated rewards, visual on own performance, awareness of the ability to self-improve as well as improved morale.

LINKS BETWEEN PERFORMANCE APPRAISAL AND CAREER DEVELOPMENT

To fully understand the context of the link, each of these processes will be explained before demonstrating the mutual link between them.

Performance appraisal is a review and discussion of an employee's performance of allocated tasks and responsibilities and based on results gathered by methods directly related to the employee's job and not the employee's personality characteristics. The appraisal measures skills and performance and identifies skills that can be leveraged, and skills that need to be improved with additional training[24]. Whereas career development is defined as a lifelong process of managing life, learning and work and involves planning and decision making with regards to education, training, and career choices, as well and developing the skills and knowledge to ensure this[58].

One of the core purposes of a performance appraisal is career development, as it identifies which of the employee's stronger abilities and skills can be leveraged, and which of the employee's lesser competencies can be improved with training. Performance appraisals can lead to identifying possible employees for succession planning and promotion[59].

Performance appraisal in career development leads to the recognition of the performance of the employee and their contribution to the organization; this usually takes on the form of rewards or promotion. Performance appraisal further helps in identifying the hidden talents and potentials of an employee which could help prepare the employee for higher responsibilities and positions[60].

Performance appraisal and career development can be the most meaningful to the organization and its employees when these two processes draw strengths of each other. e.g.: The "now" factor of performance appraisal, versus the "future" orientation of career development. In order to leverage the benefits of this mutually strengthening process, the two systems must be grouped within the same organizational goal of talent management[61]. This goal involves promoting employees' skills and knowledge. Focusing on the current performance as well as future contributions can lead to achieving this goal and organizations should leverage historic performance data to contribute to achieving this goal. The role of the human resource professional is that of a change agent and facilitator in attaining the match between appraisal and career development. When career development and performance appraisal are viewed as supporting each other, then the result is in fact stronger[62].

Simply:

Career development and performance appraisal do not have to form a tight bond, and can, in fact, be done at different times and by different people, however, mutual respect should be maintained, and shared objectives should be recognized. Forming a closer relationship between the two processes paves the way for managers to be more involved in the career development and employees in performance appraisals.

There is an intrinsic link between the outcomes of the performance appraisal process and inputs of the career development process.

About The Author

Jan H Pieterse is the founder of *NextCEO*, a member of Mensa, serial entrepreneur, specialist software engineer and the author of various business and information technology related articles. He has authored various other articles under pen names. He lives in Centurion, South Africa with his wife and two sons. With almost two decades of hands-on experience, he is a veteran in the information technology field. Entrepreneurship, business management, and leadership have always been at the forefront of his aspirations. He was a co-founder of various companies and has contributed and consulted on business development and strategic processes of several of organizations.

Learn more about Jan H Pieterse at NextCEO.co.za

OTHER BOOKS BY JAN H PIETERSE

At the time of publishing this edition of the book, I am in process of authoring the following books, please go to my website nextceo.co.za and sign up your details and I will send you a personal email when they are published:

- The Simple Side of Human Resource Management
- The Simple Side of Financial Management
- The Simple Side of Strategic Management
- The Simple Side of Marketing Management
- The Simple Side of Project Management
- The Simple Side of Economics
- The Simple Side of Negotiation and Conflict Management
- The Simple Side of Information, Communication and Technology Management

You can get all my books on my Author Central page:

Jan H Pieterse http://amzn.to/2esEZOd

One Last Thing

If you enjoyed this book or found it useful I'd be very grateful if you'd post a short review on Amazon. Your support really does make a difference and I read all the reviews personally so I can get your feedback and make this book even better.

If you'd like to leave a review then all you need to do is click the review link on this book's page on Amazon here:

Review here: http://amzn.to/2dwJSBE

Thank you again for your support!

Bibliography

1. Weinberger, LA (1998) Commonly held theories of human resource development, Human Resource Development International
2. Heathfield, S.M. (2012a), What is Human Resource Management? About.com, viewed 9 May 2012, <http://humanresource.about.com/od/glossaryh/f/hr_management.htm>.
3. Milkovich, G.T & Newman, J.M. (2002) Compensation. 7th ed. New York: McGraw-Hill.
4. Du Toit, G.S. Erasmus, B.J. & Strydom, J.W. (Eds.) (2010) Introduction to Business Management. 8th ed. Cape Town: Oxford University Press.
5. Guilford, D, & Hubbard, A 1995, Taking a systematic approach, Mortgage Banking, 55, 7, p. 65, Business Source Elite, EBSCOhost, viewed 19 July 2012.
6. Alfus, P (2000), Today's recruitment practices require traditional and Internet techniques, Hotel & Motel Management, 215, 20, p. 70, Business Source Elite, EBSCOhost, viewed 24 July 2012.
7. Lee, S. (2012) The Five Stages of Team Development. EzineArticles.com, viewed 9 May 2012, <http://ezinearticles.com/?The-Five-Stages-of-Team-Development&id=1254894>.
8. Group Dynamics (2006) In: Helms, M.M. (Ed.) Encyclopaedia of Management. Farmington Hills, MI: Gale Cengage. [Accessed online] Viewed 9 May 2012, <http://www.enotes.com/management-encyclopedia/group-dynamics>.
9. Papa, J. (2012) Importance of Effective Communication in Leadership. eHow.com, viewed 26 July 2012, <http://www.ehow.com/way_5746380_importance-effective-communication-leadership.html>.
10. Barrett, D.J. (2006), A Communication Approach for Senior-Level Managers, Handbook of Business Strategy,p.385 - 390, Rice University, Houston, Texas: Emerald Group Publishing.
11. Dowd-Krause, A. (2009). An optimal skills development planning and implementation process flow model for local government. Nelson Mandela Metropolitan University Business School
12. Heathfield, S.M. (2012b), 360 Degree Feedback
13. Dictionary.com (2012), hallo effect, viewed 01 Aug 2012, <http://dictionary.reference.com/browse/halo+effect>
14. Merriam-Webster (2012), halo effect, viewed 01 Aug 2012, <http://www.merriam-webster.com/dictionary/halo%2Beffect>
15. Management Study Guide (MSG) (2012), Performance Appraisal Tools and Techniques, viewed 01 Aug 2012, <http://www.managementstudyguide.com/performance-appraisal-tools.htm>
16. Muchinsky, P. M. (2006), Psychology applied to work. 8th ed, Belmont, CA: Thomson Wadsworth.
17. Investopedia. (2013). Human Resource Planning - HRP. Retrieved 07 08, 2013, from Investopedia: http://www.investopedia.com/terms/h/human-resource-planning.asp

18. HRcouncil. (2013). HR Planning. Retrieved 07 08, 2013, from Hrcouncil.ca: http://hrcouncil.ca/hr-toolkit/planning-strategic.cfm
19. Sullivan, D. J. (2010, 05 10). The Steps of the Recruiting Process . Retrieved 07 08, 2013, from ERE.net: http://www.ere.net/2010/05/10/the-steps-of-the-recruiting-process-%E2%80%A6-and-how-to-identify-failure-points/
20. Hendricks, K., & Louw-Potgieter, J. (2012). A theory evaluation of an induction programme. SA Journal of Human Resource Management.
21. Harvey, R. J., Dunnette, M. D., & Hough, L. M. (1991). Handbook of industrial and organizational psychology. In R. J. Harvey, M. D. Dunnette, & L. M. Hough, Handbook of industrial and organizational psychology (Vol. Vol. 2 (2nd ed.), pp. 71-163). Palo Alto: Consulting Psychologists Press.
22. Dessler, G. (2011). Human Resource Management. Prentice Hall.
23. Regenesys. (2013). Human Resource Management II Study Guide. Johannesburg: Regenesys.
24. Worcester Polytechnic Institute. (2013). Performance Reviews. Retrieved 08 08, 2013, from Worcester Polytechnic Institute: http://www.wpi.edu/offices/hr/performance.html
25. Management Study Guide (M.S.G.). (2013b). Compensation Management. Retrieved 07 08, 2013, from Managementstudyguide.com: http://www.managementstudyguide.com/compensation-management.htm
26. Humancapitalmanagement.com. (2013). Factors Affecting Human Capital Management. Retrieved 07 15, 2013, from Human capital management: http://www.humancapitalmanagement.co.za/factors-affecting-human-capital-management/
27. Rouse, M. (2012, 04). Human Capital Management (HCM). Retrieved 07 15, 2013, from Techtarget.com: http://searchfinancialapplications.techtarget.com/definition/human-capital-management
28. Baron, A., & Armstrong, M. (2007). Human Capital Management: Achieving Added Value Through People. London: Kogan Page.
29. Foot, M., & Hook, C. (2011). Introducing Human Resource Management, 6/E. London: Financial Times/ Prentice Hall.
30. Swanepoel, B. (ed.), Erasmus, B. & Schenk, H. (2008) South African Human Resource Management. 4th edition. Cape Town: Juta.
31. Brian J. Smith, J. W. (2006). Human resource planning. Human Resource Management, 81-93.
32. CIPD. (2012, 08). Workforce planning. Retrieved 07 15, 2013, from CIPD: http://www.cipd.co.uk/hr-resources/factsheets/workforce-planning.aspx
33. Wyatt, W. (2012). Workforce planning. Retrieved 07 15, 2013, from McGill - Human Resources: http://www.mcgill.ca/hr/workforce-planning
34. Brunot, T. (2013). What Is a Gap Analysis for Human Resources? Retrieved 08 04, 2013, from Small Business by Demand Media: http://smallbusiness.chron.com/gap-analysis-human-resources-61949.html
35. Stratagyn Inc. (2013). HR Gap Analysis. Retrieved 08 04, 2013, from Stratagyn HR Consulting: http://www.stratagyn.com/hrgap_analysis.html

36. Dubey, A. (2013). Gap Analysis Of Human Resources. Retrieved 08 04, 2013, from citeHR: http://www.citehr.com/421394-gap-analysis-hr-human-resources.html
37. CTMRG. (2013). Human Resource Gap Analysis or Audit. Retrieved 08 04, 2013, from Connecticut Manufacturers Resource Group: http://mmrgct.com/?page_id=388
38. Precision Labour. (2005, 12 05). Blue Sky Region HR Gap Analysis of four industries. Retrieved 08 04, 2013, from Blue Sky Net: `www.blueskyegc.ca/HR%20Gap%20Analysis%20-%20Blue%20Sky%20-%20Dec%202005%20-%20FINAL.pdf
39. Heathfield, S. M. (2013). Job Description. Retrieved 08 04, 2013, from About.com: http://humanresources.about.com/od/jobdescriptions/g/job_description.htm
40. Simplicity HR. (2013). The Importance of Succession Planning. Retrieved 08 04, 2013, from SimplicityHr.com: http://www.simplicityhr.com/resources/articles/strategies/succession
41. Creative Leading. (2013). The Importance of Succession Planning. Retrieved 08 04, 2013, from Innovative Business Resources: http://www.creativeleading.com/succession.html
42. Rothwell, W. J. (2009). Ten Key Steps to Effective Succession Planning. Pennsylvania: Rothwell and Associates.
43. Rothwell, W. J. (2005). Succession Planning 3/E. New York: American Management Association.
44. Wolfe, M. (2013). What Role Does Job Analysis Play in Effective Strategic Staffing? Retrieved 08 04, 2013, from Small Business by Demand Media: http://smallbusiness.chron.com/role-job-analysis-play-effective-strategic-staffing-13717.html
45. Management Study Guide (M.S.G.). (2013c). Job Analysis and Strategic HRM. Retrieved 08 04, 2013, from Management Study Guide: http://www.managementstudyguide.com/job-analysis-strategic-hrm.htm
46. Agrawala, K. (2010, 04 18). What the difference is between pay and/or reward system in any company. Retrieved 08 04, 2013, from Enotes.com: http://www.enotes.com/homework-help/what-difference-between-pay-reward-system-any-157897
47. WiseGeek. (2013). What Is the Difference Between Salary and Remuneration. Retrieved 08 04, 2013, from WiseGeek: http://www.wisegeek.com/what-is-the-difference-between-salary-and-remuneration.htm
48. Kohn, A. (1987, 01 19). Creativity and intrinsic interest diminish if task is done for gain. Retrieved 08 05, 2013, from Naggum.no: http://naggum.no/motivation.html
49. Schultz, W. (2002, 10 10). Getting Formal with Dopamine and Reward. Neuron, 241-263.
50. Bolton, D. (2013, 05 28). The Importance and Benefits of Employee Rewards and Recognition. Retrieved 08 05, 2013, from Yahoo Voices: http://voices.yahoo.com/the-importance-benefits-employee-rewards-and-12150118.html?cat=3

51. Wright, C. S. (2007). Hierarchy of Needs and the Total Reward System. Journal of Dental Technology, 21.
52. Lawler, E. E., & Jenkins, G. D. (1992). Strategic Reward Systems. CEO Publications, 9-10.
53. Martinez, D. V. (2013). What is the Value of Using Performance Management. UK: Centre for Business Performance, Cranfield School of Management.
54. Management Study Guide (M.S.G.). (2013a). Benefits of a Performance Management System. Retrieved 08 08, 2013, from Managementstudyguide.com: http://www.managementstudyguide.com/benefits-of-performance-management-system.htm
55. Jean. (2013). What are the benefits of performance management. Retrieved 08 07, 2013, from YoExpert: http://management.yoexpert.com/management-skills/what-are-the-benefits-of-performance-management-fo-778.html
56. Davis, P., & Rogers, R. W. (2013). Getting the most from your performance management system. Development Dimensions International.
57. Pulakos, E. D. (2009). Performance Management: A New Approach for Driving Business Results. West Sussex: John Wiley & Sons, Ltd.
58. DEEWR. (2013). Career Development. Retrieved 08 08, 2013, from Department of Education, Employment and Workplace Relations - Australian Government: http://deewr.gov.au/career-development
59. Poonacha, R. (2011, 09 07). Human Resource Planning and Human Resource Audit. Retrieved 08 08, 2013, from SlideShare: http://www.slideshare.net/SiddheshLakhan/performance-apraisal
60. Naukrihub. (2013). Performance Appraisals as Career Development. Retrieved 08 08, 2013, from Naukrihub: http://appraisals.naukrihub.com/appraisal-and-career-development.html
61. Sharma, S., Singh, S., Singh, P., & Singh, P. (2012). Performance Appraisal and Career Development. VSRD International Journal of Business & Management Research, 8-16.
62. Jacobson, B., & Kaye, B. (1986, 01). Career Systems International. Retrieved 08 08, 2013, from Career Systems International: http://careersystemsintl.org/PDF%20Files/Career%20Development%20and%20Performance%20Appraisal%20-%20It%20Takes%20Two%20to%20Tango.pdf
63. Mintzberg, H. (1973). The Nature of Managerial Work. New York: Harper & Row.

www.ingramcontent.com/pod-product-compliance
Lightning Source LLC
Chambersburg PA
CBHW061449180526